Goodnight Just The Same

Written by
April Claxton

Illustrated by
Diane Koziol Krueger

Edited by
Marissa Cohen

Author's dedication:

This book is dedicated to Madison and Heather. To Madison because you have given me the greatest gift and opportunity to experience love and live life by being your mommy. And to Heather for showing me that after the rain there will always be a rainbow. You have taught me that love and respect can be found in the same place and that all dreams are worth going after. Thank you both for being my family.   And to Hudson, KJ, Gio, Gabriana, Logan, Leah, Nicky, Emily and Brenna- You are the beautiful stars that light my way today, tomorrow and forever. You ARE great and I believe in you. I love you. You make our family so wonderful .   ~April Claxton

Illustrator's dedication:

These drawings are dedicated to my three children; Claire, Adam and Sophie, who because of my life choices, now experience several of the family situations represented in this book. Their unconditional love allows them to see the best in every situation and they continue to be amazingly strong and kind freespirits.

~Diane Koziol Krueger

For more copies of Goodnight Just The Same go to:

www.createspace.com/3530872

Goodnight Just The Same
© 2011 April Claxton

The Movement Within,
Fort Lauderdale, FL

www.themovementwithin.com

Why I wrote this book:

Each night we go to sleep. We brush our teeth, get into our jammies and tuck our daughter into bed. Each night I look at the moon and thank God for another day that I was able to live and experience my family. It really is all about love. I was raised with a step-father and step-brothers and no matter what, that was my family. Although it was "different," it was still mine. I remember when I was little asking the moon to watch over my daddy while I was at my mom's house and my dad was at his. Now, as I am older and have a little one of my own who has her own step-parents, it is important to stress to her that it matters not what or who a family is made up of. What does matter is the amount of love that exists within the family. The good feelings matter. The respect and joy matters and it doesn't matter if there is a mommy and daddy, two mommies or two daddies or no mommy or no daddy, a child is loved at all times and the moon tucks everyone in just the same.

— April xoxo

Away goes the sun
and jumps into bed.
It
SQUiGGLES
and
GiGGLES
as it covers its head.

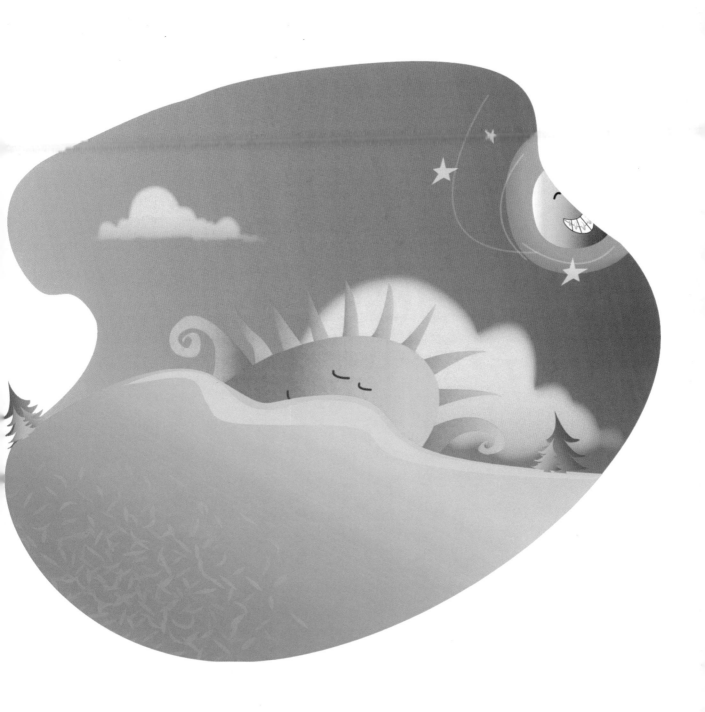

2

Out comes the moon

full of smiles

and

LIGHT.

It shines as it lines up

the stars in

the

NIGHT.

The babies are happy

as they coo

iN

their sleep.

They cuddle and snuggle

THEiR

soft cuddly

sheep.

The big kids dream
of the day that
is
done.
They know that
tomorrow will
BRING
them more fun.

8

The mommies and daddies

sleep to the songs of

THEIR

hearts–

Whether in bed

with each other or

DREAMING

apart.

The step-mommies
and
STEP-DADDIES
have gone to sleep
too–
KNOWING
how lucky they are
to have you.

The pets are
all cozy
snuggled by the
BRIGHTEST
moonbeams.
They swim and they jump
as they play in
THEIR
dreams.

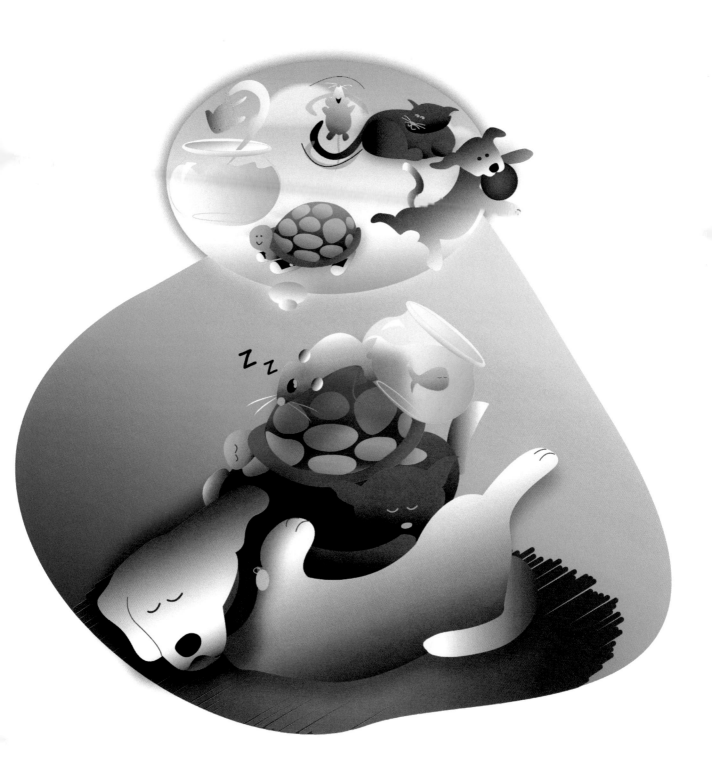

14

Either asleep

or awake,

a family is made of one

THING.

It is not

the people or type,

but the love that they

BRING.

No matter the
FAMILY
and who or what
they are made of,
A family's a
FAMILY
when they all
come from love.

To the moon

there's no difference

iN

your place or your name,

For each

NiGHT

every family is tucked in

just the same.

Place a photo of your own
fabulously unique family here!

About the author:

April Claxton is the CEO and founder of The Movement Within.com and is a motivational speaker and author. She writes messages of hope and inspiration and orchestrates classes, workshops and The Movement Within Radio to help children and adults discover the magic and necessity of self. She is a surviving victim of domestic violence and abuse and has made it her life's mission to teach others how important and perfect they really are.

April enjoys spending her free time with her daughter and partner in South Florida where they travel, go to the beach to hunt for shells and treasures and run around chasing their chihuahua-pug, Shamu.

About the illustrator:

Diane Koziol Krueger is the CEO, founder and brand identity expert at Contagiousllc.com. Art as been a part of her life since she could pick up a crayon and self-love is her most recent appreciation. Combining these two passions, Diane now helps other businesses promote their messages of life, love and self awareness.

Diane currently resides in Novi, Michigan with her three children, two cats and one big enthusiasm for life. Diane spends her free time doing yoga, cycling and attending inspiring events for her blog Fine ART Friday.

Another inspiring book from April Claxton

THE MOVEMENT
WITHIN:
8 STEPS TO IGNITE THE
MOVEMENT WITHIN YOU

REGAINING YOUR LIFE,
YOUR POWER, YOUR SELF

APRIL
CLAXTON

When we move within, we begin. We use our past and experiences to learn about who we are. We discover and learn to accept and love ourselves. We learn that we are ready and able to live happily, freely and completely.

Life requires movement. Growth requires movement. This book is intended to give you the steps and direction required to help you create this movement.

You will understand where you've been, appreciate where you are and find the desire to create where it is you want to be. Life starts within. Change starts within. Within is where you begin.

By applying and practicing these steps, you can regain your life, discover yourself and empower who you magically already are.

This is YOUR life, YOUR movement, YOUR time. Let YOUR movement begin!

www.themovementwithin.com

The Movement Within: 8 Steps To Ignite The Movement Within You
can be found at **www.createspace.com/3511540**

Made in the USA
Las Vegas, NV
21 October 2021